# LET US DANCE!

## THE STUMBLE & WHIRL WITH THE BELOVED

Poetry

by

Chelan Harkin

*To your radiance.
Love,
Chelan*

# DEDICATION

To Mary Reed

# CONTENTS

# ACKNOWLEDGMENTS

I acknowledge with love every single minuscule and magnificent force that has ever impacted this Universe and to all life that has ever been animated to dance its existence on this Earth— Certainly, in some way, on some level, it's all played a role. Now that we've covered that...

With great love I thank my husband, Noah, for his multilayered support, both practical and emotional. He is the safe harbor where my poems first go for the kiss of encouragement before they head out to the big, wide world. His wonderful heart beams so much loving strength into me on the daily.

To my sweet, luminous kids, Amari and Nahanni. You keep me tethered to this world. If not for you I might just float off into some ethereal poetry realm and never come back! And you also are my primary motivation to grow into the finest version of myself that I might.

To Daniel Ladinsky, a great poetic inspiration and a wonderful encourager and edifier of my writing who has also provided inspiration for my cover with his simple and elegant designs.

Another shout out to my dear friend, Mary Reed, who has become one of my greatest sunshines.

To Laurel Fitzhugh for her generous and fantastic web design support...www.chelanharkin.com—check it out!

To Anita Johnston, one of my all time favorite authors whose one of a kind book, Eating In The Light Of The Moon, is a bible of empowerment and transformation for women. Thank you for putting your insightful voice into the foreword for this book.

To Jordan Blummer for her extraordinary cover design—am I right?!? And she's available for more work: blumerjordan@gmail.com

To the matriarchs of my family, my grandmothers, Violet Knight (Gram) and Dorothy Weiler (Nano). Both have nourished me in too many ways to mention.

To all of my Facebook darlings. You are my poetry's chorus of incredible encouragement and the midwives of this book. I consider you all dear friends. It would both be fun and tedious as hell to even try to list you all but I sure hope you know who you are.

# FOREWORD

The feminine is emerging into our consciousness. For far too long she has been dismissed, denied, devalued, and degraded. We are now living in a time when she is breaking free of her genderized chains so she can be discovered deep within the heart of all of us. While she has been ever present, we are now turning to her, consciously and deliberately, to listen to the song she has sung since time immemorial. In doing so we can become aware of her as a force we can commune with and turn to for guidance and healing.

Chelan gives poetic, lyrical voice to the ineffable energetic constellation of the ancient feminine, with all her fierce tenderness, so we can embrace her and come into her embrace, no longer separate and estranged from this powerful life force. She lends her words so we can hear her call, attune to her message, reflect upon the beauty of her light, and celebrate her awe-inspiring presence.

Indeed, the feminine is here. The words on these pages invite you to listen with your inner ear and dance to the rhythm of her beating heart.

Anita Johnston, Ph.D

Author, *Eating in the Light of the Moon*

# THE AUDACIOUS GOAL

My poetry has

the audacious goal

to take your breath

away

that you might stop,

even for that moment,

taking it for granted

and want it back.

My poetry has

the audacious goal

to stop you in the tracks

of your busy life,

even briefly,

and help you fall

from your unstable worship

of cerebral gods

back into the soft bed

of your heart.

My poetry has

the audacious goal

to remind you,

if only for a breath,

that there's loveliness

built into you

that's more intimate and essential

than even your DNA

and my poetry has the audacious goal

of inviting itself into you

to ring that bell of remembrance.


My poetry desires to be

a sacred interruption!

To remove the veil

if only for a glimpse

that you may consider

how perfectly set the jewel of our earth is

in relation to the golden amulet of the sun

and the similar relationship

between our hearts

and God.

My poetry has the audacious goal

to grab a handful

of God

and, if only for an instant,

gift that back

to your heart.

# READ MY POEMS

Read my poems
as though they're written
to you—
they are.


My demographic is hearts.
If you find something in my poetry
that brings nourishment
to the sweet lips
of your soul,
or that quenches a thirst
know there is no question
that cup
was placed there
for you.


In fact, whatever your heart
was longing for
is probably what inspired these poems

4

in the first place.

# I DON'T KNOW WHAT TO CALL IT

I don't know what to call it

so I call it God:

that exquisite flowering of every

piece of me I had once

relegated to the shadows

or what happens

when poetry

opens its fist

in my heart

setting light free.

The seed didn't know what to call it either,

This Song,

This Relationship,

This thing that led

to the exquisite unfoldment

of its own Nameless Self.

If you come up

with a better name,

let me know.


Until then I'll call it God,

that One who moves me to dip

the cup of consciousness

into the waters

of existence

and whispers

from every ordinary,

precious moment,


"drink deep."

# STOP THINKING ABOUT GOD

Stop thinking about God—

cry your heart out.


Stop your dry, prim talks with God—

She doesn't desire

those boring meetings.


Wake up at midnight

and write Her love poems

with star ink.


God's tired of the same position

with prayer


lie down on the forest floor

and drink Her in

through your pores.


Stop waiting for Her

to give your deeds golden stars

and realize you are made of them.

# THE THING THAT MAKES YOUR HEART SING

The thing that makes

your heart sing

might be quirky as hell,

it might not do anything for capitalism,

no one might buy it.


You've probably written this thing off

countless times

for those reasons

and because you probably should

do the dishes or something more practical

like that instead.


But this thing that makes your heart sing

is the thing inside of you that most wants

to topple your kingdom of shoulds

that wants deeply and burningly

to be prioritized

and for no particular reason

but that it brings so much light.


It wants to look you straight in the eye

and say, "Let's do this, baby!"

even if it's drilling holes in seashells and stringing them to

fishing line,

even if it's drawing anatomical pictures of a flower

with great care that are never meant

to be hung in an art gallery

but to be pressed

into the precious pages of your heart,


even if it's making a new kind of cookie

each week

and devouring them with relish on your couch

by yourself,

a sweet sacrament

just meant to share

with your taste buds.

This thing that makes your heart sing

will resurrect parts of your life

and restore a sacred nutrient

to your days.


It can be muted

but never silenced.

If you're not sure what it is,

just listen for the reoccurring whispers

in your chest

of that flame that will not die.


The paradox is this:

while the thing itself might seem simple,

this thing that makes

your heart sing

will create a luminosity

so bright

you'll be the envy

of all the stars

and they'll want to jump into

your body

to feel it.

# WOMAN CHURCH

It's time for Woman Church.

Here, we enter the pews
in the heart
and listen to the sermon
of our hips.

We worship the holy trinity:
Maiden, Mother, Crone.

The softness of our bodies
is our primary temple,
we revere
curves and plentifulness
and dance to celebrate it,
if we like.

Our sacrament is seconds
on everything we desire

and here

we heap our plates.


We delight in the holy doctrine

of supporting deep nourishment

and singing sacred praise

to our sisters.


We tell our stories

and braid each other's hair

while we pray

sitting in a circle

announcing our power,

our tenderness,

our beauty,

our voices,

our grief.


We invite the ancestors in

for tea

and bring all cast-out feelings

in from the cold.

We paint pictures

of Goddess relaxing

and taking a much needed break

while gods massage her feet

with oils

and feed her grapes.

# I AM DONE

God, I am done
with small, meek prayers.

I feel a surging ocean
of light within me
and I would like it
to flood the world.

You've placed enough
gifts in me to satisfy eternity
I would like them brought forth
and unwrapped.

I am done playing small.

I want my poetry
to soar high enough
to kiss the sun
and share stories of light

with the world.

Why would I not ask
for my own greatness
to be pulled forth
like a tree from a seed?

I'm done thinking it unseemly
to ask precisely
for the vastness of desires
You've placed in my chest
to show themselves.

I am a temple holding You.
It seems it would bring joy
to the both of us
to make Your mysteries and delights
reveal themselves through me
and I am ready.

I am the boldness of a Universe
that knows its potential

is uncontainable

and I'm ready to expand

into unseen wondrous realms

of my own Self.


I am ready to receive

Your astonishment

of all I might unfold

to be.


I am ready to put myself forward

and see

how Great Beauty might rise

to meet me.

# I AM TOO MUCH!

It's time to reframe

and reclaim

the phrase,

"I am too much"

It's time to practice

being okay with it

lathering ourselves in it

and basking in all

that we are—

Here goes:

I'm too much!

I want to devour suns

for breakfast

and kiss the center

of every heart.

I'm too much

for niceties.

All I want

is to experience

the inmost nectar

of the soul.


I'm too much!

I'm divorcing myself

from the timid,

ongoingly gray life

of a repressed sky—

let's dive in

to the center of our storms!


I'm too much

for small ideologies

to encourage me to live

in the margins of the heart

on the outside of life.


I'm too much

to be appropriately tipsy.

I want to pop the cork

off this world

and make all things

intoxicated with glee!


I'm too much!

I want to stalk God

all the way home

to the center of every beauty

and sweetness.


Go forth, glorious

"too much" ones

and pour your rivers of light

that quench the world.


Go forth and feed

every ravenous soul

from the generous table

of your heart

knowing your essence is one

of feast,

not famine.

Go forth and live

in a way that reminds people

how abundantly luminous

each night is,

bedecked in her stars.

Let your too muchness

be your devotion—

God, after all,

is the Queen of Too Much,

polyamorous with every religion

and every heart as She is

and She does not stop

making her point

after only one galaxy.

Yes by all means

be too much!

Your heart was made

to be a gong

not a penny whistle


Your beauty is a downpour

not a sprinkle.


Your voice is a nourishing meal

for this hungry world

not a garnish.


"You're too much"

has been a tight judgment

that tries to tie down

your vastness

and constrain the cosmos

within you—


reclaim it and pour forth

your stars,


reclaim it and become just the right size

to hold the Universe.

# THE GOD WHO MADE THE OCTOPUS

If you think

the Eccentric God who made

the octopus

is gonna judge you

for your sins,

I'm afraid you've missed

the mark.


If you think this

Wild God

that spins galaxies

as a pastime

cares to get fussy

about your mistakes,

or has ever made anything

that wasn't born

perfect and luminous,

you might need to repent.

If you can't yet admit

how lovable

and infinitely worthy

the fullness of your human nature is,

and if you think God

wants to do anything

but perpetually pour

an abundance

of love gifts

upon you,

well, my dear, your soul

just might need

to go to confession.

# MAKE YOUR LOVE VISIBLE

God had a great secret

that She just couldn't keep

and one day

Her Heart exploded

with the Big Bang.

Her inability to contain Herself

became galaxies.

She poured Her Heart out

and it slowly began

sorting itself out

into the Universe.

She spilled the beans (the stars)

so completely,

Her repressed blushing

became sunsets,

She whispered Her secret music

into the heart of every atom

and the electrons

could not help

but giddily dance.

All creation became a chatter box,

gossiping to each other nonstop,

about the wild, loving mysteries

She'd shared with them.

Evolution was what happened

as the story of ecstatic wonderment

was passed through life

from ear to ear,

changing slightly

with each iteration.

She set truth to dancing

with the whirl of Her planets

and kissed the nucleus of everything

with her only real ordinance:


"Make your love visible."

# ORIGIN STORY

There's a God who made the clitoris

and extreme pleasure—

let's not marginalize those facts.


There's a God who made honey and nectar and pollen

and bees

who live their whole lives practicing high levels of P.D.A.

with flowers—

let's not forget that either.


There's a God who made all humans

originate from a beautiful Black woman

in the heart of Africa—

no need to white wash that.


There's a God who made hips that respond

to music—

I mean, that wasn't an accident, right?

There's a God who made a system

for each being to be created

from the great act of love and pleasure—

can our toilsome ways

remember those origins?


Consider this poem

a short sermon

to allow the vibrant, fertile

wholeness of our truth back in,

to let our inherent God given verve return

to sauce up our souls.


I think if we became a bit less

selectively forgetful

and let ourselves remember all of this

church would get

a whole lot more interesting.

# THE FEMININE IS HERE

The Feminine is here
to crack open your body,
women AND men
and finally release the poison
of every ancient, uncleaned wound.

The Feminine is here
to crack open your old ideologies
and shoot new life through you
like a seed
hard and closed for so many years
and suddenly kissed into transformation
by the great destruction
of light.

The Feminine is here to pull you
from the measured, surveyed land
at the edge
of the wild forest

of your dreams

and finally toss you

into the map-less territory

of your heart.


The Feminine is here

to lay your impressive

certificates of learning

at the feet of inner knowing,


to pluck you from the discipleship

of an outward master

and lay you at the altar

of your inner truth,


and to activate this inner truth

that has long been waiting latent

and so eager to erupt

from your soul.


The Feminine is here

to remind you that God

can live in the earth, in the hips

in the deepest shadows,


that She is planted

like a wild rose

in the darkest

furrows

of your pain,

to reteach you

to mother your frailties

rather than dominate them

and bring the wound from exile

into embrace.


The Feminine is here to bring you home

just as you are now,

to undo conditions

around enoughness,

to undo every patriarchal corset

cinched around your voice and spirit

and return you to the full belly

of your sacred breath.

The Feminine is here to reunite

tenderness with power,

to help you source this

from the great, hidden sea within,

and for you to feel the intimacy of God

pulsing Her embodied song

through the rivers of your blood

and back to the holy ocean

of your heart.


The Feminine is here to tell us

in no uncertain terms

we are carrying new wisdom,

a gestation of God

in the womb of our consciousness,


and a great, never before seen beauty

is soon due

to be born.

# DON'T TRAP GOD IN CHURCH

Don't trap God in church,

in any mosque or temple—

don't chain Him to Sundays.


Give God the Universal Passport

to let Him move beyond

the borders of any one religion.


Set Him free from living in the sky,

from the limitations

of only dwelling in light—

even that gets stuffy.


Of course let's not confine God

to a gender role

no one needs the trappings

of that old business.


God is more flexible

than rules,

more beautiful and fluid

than rightness,

more whole

than just holy,

more inclusive

than purely pure.


Let your spiritual path be

taking up the guerrilla mission

to pass the sacred keys

to every leaf, tree, plant, flower,

every beautiful movement,

every person you meet,


so that God may be unlocked

from all things

and come forward to greet you

from every little beauty

and shadow in this world.


There's only one dance-hall

in this Universe

wide enough to accommodate the breadth

and sprawling beauty

of this Divine Dance—

are you ready to get

this whole world whirling?


Free yourself from every mental trapping

and place God in your heart.

# THE SOUL'S HOMELAND

Sometimes my soul

feels itself

to be in great exile

from its homeland,

but then I remember

my mother tongue

is the poetry

my heart is so fluent in,

its dialect,

laughter and tears.

My other native language

is rising early

to praise all the great things

the sun falls upon.

My national song

is a geyser of joy

hitting the highest notes

of ecstasy

and breaking every glass ceiling

in the mind

that once trapped God inside.


My anthem is the feisty love parade

that marches gaily from my heart

to yours.


My religion is the untying

of old knots

that once kept my soul hitched

to rigidity and smallness,


and my doctrine

is whatever comes after that,

when the soul's full range

of movement is restored.


My flag is every mood

of the moon

that reflects my inmost heart

My ancestry is the collection
of radiance
from morning dew
passed down by blades of grass
as they stand vigil
in silent reverence
to be part of each morning's inheritance
of such wonder,

My DNA is the encrypted love notes
written in the luminous ink
from the stars.

My soul is an ancient heritage
of love songs from God,
and whatever it is I'm doing here
has mostly to do
with pledging allegiance
to this glorious anthem.
Whatever I'm doing here

has mostly to do

with expressing my devotion

for the borderless birthplace

deep in my chest,


where beauty again and again

takes her first breath.

# THIS IS A FEELING UNIVERSE

This is a feeling Universe.


Do you think the flower opens

for intellectual reasons?


Or does it have more to do

with needing to finally feel

the kiss of the sun

in the center

of her wide open heart?


Sweet pea, it is the same for you.

What is the source sweet enough

to beckon you

to begin that sacred process

of opening

that brings your love forward?

What is that kiss

that entices you beyond yourself,

that you simply cannot

do without?

# YOU CAN EVICT GOD

You can choose

to evict God


from His snooty sky nest

at any time,

and re-home Him

in the cozy burrow of your chest.


You can choose

to open to the Great She-God

and experience The Mother in every pore.


You can choose to disarm God

of all His weapons,

take away His hardest sticks

of judgment and conditionality,

and finally just breathe love.


You can choose to relieve

stern, perfectionist, hard-ass God

from His duties

that have been serving no one

and go with a new boss

(or better yet, Friend)

who has the qualities on His resume

you might actually want:


Authentic, Close, Open, Humorous, So Sweet.

You can let go of absent

and know that God desires you too!

And all of this great change begins,

whenever you're brave enough

to choose it,


right in the softest center

of your own heart.

# I'M STARTING TO THINK IT JUST
# MIGHT BE REAL

In spite of our insistence

that we believe in God,


in spite of our hard commitments,

our whole collection

of sworn oaths

and solemn vows,

our trove of prostrations,

our stack of prayers,

the truth is,


if we had one real taste

of The Great Wild One,

that Extraordinary Creator

that made the octopus, the persimmon,

that created these hearts

that can somehow

contain the whole universe—

well, we'd be totally done for.


Our lives would be turned

on their heads,

this world would be poured out

and every orderly way

would be consumed by this Sun.


If we just started to think,

"All of this just might be real"

Midas would touch your heart

and turn everything

golden,


right and wrong

would be gloriously dethroned

from your mind

in the great fall of everything

christened and transformed

into holy song,


every dispute about

sacred and profane,

all structures coming

from naught,

every fear of ultimate aloneness

that plays out its terrors

on the whole world,

every tantrum about wondering

if this love is big enough

to even reach us

would be undone

by this kiss.


Every deed done

as an attempt to curry favor

with this One,

who fills all cups

with golden wine

regardless,

would be swept away

in bewilderment.

Every pain would be unstrung

from your beautiful

dancing heart,

every worry collapsed and dissolved

in your deepest desire

to part the lips of The Beloved

and tenderly feed Her

a taste of your sweet spirit.


Tonight the jug of the night

was pushed over,

spilling the whole collection

of stars onto my lap

and I'm starting to think

it all just might be real.

# UNTEACH ME

Unteach me

to dance—

I was born a natural.


Unteach me

vocal training—

I came here

ready to sing!


Untrain me

in the lessons of poetry—

my DNA is written in verse.


Especially undo me

from all those lessons of love—

my soul arrived

an expert.

Get out of the way pedagogy,

away with you old knowledge,

begone stale ideas—


my soul

needs space

to whirl its inbuilt joy,

to share its essential love,

to return to God,


The Most Natural

Dance.

# I TRIED TO HAGGLE GOD

I tried to haggle God

for good deeds

and a bundle of prayers—

She wasn't having it.


I tried to haggle God

for complex philosophies

and impressive recitations—

no deal.


I tried to haggle God

for following all the rules

and acting the most pure—

nothing.


I got frustrated

and was about to leave the marketplace

When she said,

"I'll trade Myself

for a diamond

of your tears,

a ruby of sorrow

from the trove of your heart,

any gem

of your joy."

# THINGS ARE ABOUT TO GET INTERESTING

Things are about to get interesting.

The more you open

to the light of the Wild Sun

the more motivated She'll be

to pour Her golden drink upon you.


You thought your life was crazy now?

Just wait until you let love in!

You think She'll bring a sip of holy wine

to your lips,

but She'll pop the cork right off

of this world

and intoxicate all existence!


Surround yourself with people

who have already been brave enough

to yank their souls

from the straight jackets

of their buds

and let the blossom

of their freak flags fly—

you will need this encouragement.


Because things are about to get interesting.

What used to be your reverent postures

will madly start trying

to pull God

into your body.


All your grounded words

will turn into the swooping birds

of unpredictable poetry

and all of your polite ways

will become true

maniacs for love.


Are you sure you're ready

to turn your respectable life

into a wild parade?

Perhaps consider this

before you pray like that

again.

# LET'S GET BUSY

What my mischievous poetry
strives to do

is pull at the loose strings
of all those false selves
you thought you were
and unravel them completely

and inspiring something
of a growing congregation
with the ecstatic innocence
of our original, holy nudeness

streak through our lives,
or at the very least,
the streets of each Sunday,
yelling, "Hallelujah!"
as God hollers a great, "Amen!"
to this wild parade!

Yes, let's get busy

with exposing our hearts

to such a degree

it makes the whole world blush.

# YOU WERE MADE TO FALL IN LOVE

Your ears,

those beautiful, tiny amphitheaters

that can hold every

dancing sound,

those perfect singing bowls

that softly

pour music through you.


Your eyes,

those fire opals,

bejeweled drops of God,

the translators

of that great romance language

of light.


Your mouth,

that holy vessel

from which every sacred sound

from your soul

can be ushered forth,

that hollow space

that vibrates ideas into shape

that gives form to love.


Your nose,

the host

to that great visitor—

the fragrance of the rose.


Your skin,

that landscape

of sensation,

a soft bed

for all touch

that covers all of you

at once.


Dear one,

God did not make you

to be rigid and follow rules.

I mean, for God's sake...

we have tongues

made of pure desire

to devour and savor

all that sweetness!


We live in a sensuous,

perfumed world—

darling, you were made

to fall in love

and this world was made

to caress you.

# IT'S ONLY A MATTER OF TIME

Dear men,

we are hairy

and we come with fat on our bodies—

does our nature repulse you?


We're hungry and we're angry

and we care

about digging up our buried wild

healing voices

beneath the dirt of the patriarchy

so that truth may again be set free—

it's all bound to be messy.


Conditioning has mis-tuned us

in that a-synchronous,

aching sound

so out of harmony

from the song of our soul.

Women want to scream

for at least as many millennia

as we've been told not to.


Our bodies change,

our moods surge,

tide-like,

we are unpredictable.


We do not march

and keep in line,

we are whirlers,


our healing is a spiral

of growth and returning,

we want to heal

not by avoiding the wound

and lusting upward

but by entering its fiery heart,

by returning to its core

and letting the molten heat

melt us to gold

We bleed as an embodied prayer

to the moon

which sings back to us the truth

of our fullness

that includes our shadow


We are done hemming our light.

It is a rough edge

frayed with darkness—

there is nothing tidy about women.


We are uncontrollable beings.

Any weakness you've detected

is a self-defense mechanism

knowing the patriarchy is too fragile

for our might.


We've been put in small boxes

and told that we're "too much"

if we expand beyond them.


Dear men, it's time

to batten down the hatches

or better yet open them wide

and ready yourself

for this Sacred Storm.


It's only a matter of time

before The Feminine,

this thrashing sea

that can only be contained

so long,

lets loose the depths and force

of Her unshakable power.

# DEAR MEN

Dear men,

just beneath our rage

lies a mountain

of profound, aching sorrow

at how far we've been

from true connection with you.


Just beneath our rage

is an ocean

of grief

at how terribly sad we are

that you haven't known

how to meet us as equals.


Just beneath our rage

lies a continent of desire

for our wholeness

to be seen, welcomed, respected, loved.

Just beneath our rage

our power

so wants to be honored,

our intelligence

so deeply wants

to be valued

and celebrated,

our feelings

to be respected,

our work

to be appreciated

and remunerated,

our voices

to be heard,

our hearts to be seen

with tender eyes,

our bodies

to be safe

and unconditionally beautiful

just as they are.


We want to love

and be loved

as full humans

and we're terribly sad

at how hard this has been.


We rage about the small spaces

we've been taught to put ourselves in

that somehow

shrinking from our fullness

might reach you.


We rage at how far we've been taught

we've had to leave ourselves

that we might find you

in our own absence.


We want you with us

in your powerful wholeness,

we want to heal with you,

we want healthy relationship,

we want tenderness,

we want power together,

we want it all—

all of us

all of you

in respect, honor and love

and we've been terribly violated

and profoundly hurt

and we need acknowledgment

and repair

we want amends

that acknowledge the depth and layered-ness

and length

of the violation

that honor what it's meant

to walk this world as a woman

so that the myriad breaches

may be bridged.


Oh, we want it to be safe enough

with you

to finally dive in together

to that ocean of grief

just beneath that rage

that unentered has set us like islands

so far apart from each other

that there might be a connective path

toward great healing

and return.


Dear men, try to understand our rage—

it hasn't happened in a vacuum.

Our pain is deep and fiery

and for a reason.

The violation and desecration

of women is ancient

and we all carry a lineage of terror,

abuse and dehumanization within us

in a wound linked to you

so vast

we barely know where

to begin entering it

though our deepest hearts

do want

to move through and beyond it

together with you

back to our nobility

back to our dignity

back to our wholeness

back to each other.

# SENSITIVE ONES

Sensitive ones,

don't be so quick

to pathologize yourself

What we call

an emotional crisis

can be truth

desperately needing to erupt

from within

and take every untrue structure

down with it.

Being called "too sensitive"

is a brutal accusation

to shame and silence

those necessary ones

who know and speak

the pain of living

in a dehumanized world.

We desperately need people

who are not okay with this

and speak to it.


Rage can be deep, fiery awareness

of so much violation

of your inherent dignity

and worth

and your mama bear soul

getting on its hind legs to roar,

"No more!"

This is a helpful asset.


Anxiety can be that

which speaks up

deep within you

when your inner light,

your tenderness,

your power,

your boundaries,

your truth,

your voice

isn't safe here—

a smart alarm bell sounding,

"Get out!"


Even your beautiful addictions

are your boldest advocates

for a spiritually sound,

wholehearted world,

that perpetually say

in no uncertain terms,

"when I hide away my love and truth

and power—I go crazy!"


Yes, dear, wise one,

don't be so quick

to pathologize yourself.

How beautiful that your body

speaks up so clearly

as a barometer for

truth, love, health and safety

and makes such a wild protest

in their absence.

# BEAUTY CONTEST

The sun and the moon

and all the stars

had a beauty contest.


Of course we know

the judges were flummoxed

and it was all a dead tie.


Beauty is incomparable—

always a perfect face

of light.


And it's the same for all of us

when looked at with sane,

healthy eyes

that can see

beneath the surface

even slightly—

darling, you will flood

all standards

when the metric becomes

how much light

you pour.

# THE GREAT CEREMONY

Bring not your pity

to the great ceremony

of another's grief.


But rather bring your honor

and celebration

to the great, sacred room

of another soul's bravery

as through their tears

they shed

the old world.


Each deep cry

is a rite of passage

that should be held as such.


Lay your reverence,

respect

and gratitude

upon the altar

of your witnessing .


You are on sanctified grounds,

you've been let in

to the temple of transformation.


What a great privilege

to witness truth

flooding another's body


Each deep cry

is a contraction

of the birth

of our new world

and each of us

is called

to do our heart's labor

to be Her mother.

# CLEANING YOUR HEART

There's crying

and then there's Crying.


Crying is the act of the true warrior,

that deep grief that cleanses the heart,

that wrings out the ancestral line

of its ancient pain,

that reaches back to the beginnings

of every oppression

you've ever known

which shares a cord with all oppression

and finally kisses even that wound

with light.


Crying allows you to dive

into and beyond the dark

that has held back countless generations

from their gifts and desires

and truths,

Crying undoes the sickness

of secrets,

Crying no longer compromises

truth for comfort,

this Crying is the evolution of the soul,

it is the alchemy of the straw

of the old world

to the gold of the new,

it is the undoing of the body

from being cinched

to the past

it unties the corset

of worn-out contracts

your soul never wanted to live in,

Crying resuscitates

your breathless life,

it is the embodied refusal

to go on serving what no longer serves you,


Crying is light

taking the shadow's hand

and courageously walking

into the Great Unknown

trusting there's wholeness

on the other side,


it is releasing once precious handholds,

it is forgoing control,

it is the time of the end

and the time of the beginning,

it dives you deep into new frontiers

that you may grab

a new handful of power,

it is surrendering deeply enough

all the structures you thought you knew

to re-home your soul in a more suitable

habitation,

Crying moves inner mountains

and slays illusion.


From the inside out

Crying undoes and remakes

the world.

# YOU DON'T HAVE TO BELIEVE IN GOD

You don't have to believe in God

but please collapse in wonder

as regularly as you can.


Try and let your knowledge

be side-swiped by awe

and let beauty be so persuasive

you find yourself willing

to lay your opinions at her feet.


Darling, you don't have to believe in God,

but please pray

for your own sake

great prayers of thanks

for the mountains, the great rivers,

the roundness of the moon

just because they're here at all

and that you get to know them

and let prayer bubble up in you

like song in a bird,

as a natural thing.


You don't have to have

a spiritual path

but do run

the most sensitive

part of your soul

over the soft curves

of this world

with as much tenderness

as you can find in yourself

and let her edge-less ways

inspire you to want to discover more.


Just find a way

that makes you want to yield

yourself

that you may be more open

to letting beauty fully

into your arms

and feel some sacred spark

inside of you that yearns toward

learning how to build a bigger

fire of love in your heart.


You don't have to believe in God

but get quiet enough to remember

we really don't know a damn thing

about any of it


and if you can, feel a reverence to be part

of This Great Something,

whatever you want to call it,

that is so much bigger

and so far beyond

the rooftops of all

of our knowing.

# A WORLD THAT INCLUDES FROGS

I am so honored

to be part of a world

that includes frogs

croaking like maniacs

from a nearby pond

for who knows what reason

though it seems for the same

impulse in my chest

that leads me to pray.


I'm so honored and dazzled

to be part of a Universe

that includes moons at all.


And who can say anything

without first being incinerated

by awe

about that great burn pile

in the sky—the sun—

that provides its own fuel

and brings everything to life

with light.


I'm so grateful

to be part of a world

that includes

the reverence of nighttime

and oceans

with unplungable depths

and hearts

yet deeper.


I'm tickled to be part of a world

that I'm certain is spun

of living poetry

and to be sewn of this same magic fabric.


I'm beyond wonderment

to stand still

within this particular twilight

while the stars appear one by one

like fireflies

turning on their lights


and know that anywhere I point

my heart's gaze

in this marvelous world

holds a full cup

of secret delight

that makes all seeking replete

with arrival.


And as my knowing lays itself

at the feet of amazement

what else can I do

but join those frogs

in their great, burbling chorus

of praise.

# TAKE A STAND

There's a story

that's been going around

called the patriarchy

that has taken

all of our breath away

in its insidious suffocation

of the truth of who we really are.

Some say this story

serves men

but it doesn't

it profoundly enables men

to stay hungry beasts

instead of soaring,

golden eagles.

And it does everything

to deny women

their inherent crowns.

This story is beyond individual men

but it can give them a pass

directly out of their humanity

onto that sick perch

of superiority

whose position must be constantly maintained

always

at the expense of women.


Dear men,

you didn't start this

but there's no need

to wait around

to be called out—


it's time we all self-diagnose

this terrible malady

of being so far

from our own hearts.


There's no need to continue

letting ancient, violent storytellers

write your lives.

Take up your pen

like the sharpest sword—

fellows, you need to start

wielding truth.


Women,

we are so much more

than what the patriarchy

has taught us we are—

we are mountains

filled with explosive light

that can dazzle the Gods

and scintillate the stars.


Men, you are so much more

than what you've learned

from the patriarchy—

you are the power

within the heart of gentleness.

You are the courage

seated on the throne

of the heart's truth

that doesn't stand down.

Now, it's time to stand up

for all of this.

## SPICE THINGS UP

You and God

have been living in the same house .

and moving around each other silently

for some time now.


Communication has been poor,

you both think the other is being distant

and hard to reach.

You're not even sharing a bed anymore!


Darling, this is when it's time to get bold—

throw a rock through your front window

and start hollering,

"something's gotta change!"

She'll respond to this feistiness.


Break all your bad vows

and undo all the contracts with stiffness

you never even really intended to sign—

you've been so perfunctory and un-creative

with the Great Wild Creator!

Stop that.


Clearly it's time to spice things up—

Shorten your skirt and tie-dye your Sunday best.


Go get some lingerie

for The Divine

and some for yourself too.


The wine bottles in the cellar of your heart

are dusty—

shine them off,

uncork the flame

of your desire

and drink that!


Wine might be too weak though,

God's no light weight.

Go deeper into the cellar of your chest

and give Her the hard stuff!

The truth is,

it only takes one gulp of soul,

one revivifying swig of truth

to rekindle the heat.


Give God a bouquet

of your verve!


Try a new position

with your prayer,


make whatever adjustments

you need

to rediscover the sweet, sweet

warmth of each other.

# IF MOTHERS RULED THE WORLD

If mothers ruled the world
all would be whole, fed and well.

War would cease,
I mean, what kind of crazy fools
send their babies to war?

Instead we would simply ask,
"how to meet that unmet need?"

The table of the world
would be set
with square meals for hearts
and all would gather round,
nourished.

The problem to solve
would be how to make
society more tender

and how do we open

all the borders

around our hearts,

that all parts of us

may have a place

for refuge.


If mothers ruled the world

we would be stewards

of the health, diversity and wild

of Mother Earth,


and each night

the stars would applaud

the beauty they witnessed here.


Magic would rise with the sun

and light

would migrate back home

to our eyes.


Creativity would pour abundantly

from humanity

like a full pitcher

of honeyed cream,


song, dance, storytelling, tribe

would not be luxuries, garnishes, dreams—

they would be as universal and essential

as our breath,


they would be the main dishes

of our lives.


There would be ceremony

around resurrecting

every unblossomed voice

as it rooted into itself

and found its flower.


There would always be circles

to hold and witness

all laughter and tears.

Deep listening

would be as requisite as taxes

and taxes would go to healing,

growing, learning, thriving, celebration.


If mothers ruled the world

this world would go

from barren to fertile,

from wasteland

to rose garden,

from revenue

to relationship,

from burned out

to powerful, full bellied flame

almost overnight


but we're tired, we're lonely,

we're malnourished

because we don't have the support

we need

because mothers do not yet

rule the world.

It's time to feed The Mother

who lives within us all.


It's time to bring

whatever nourishment we possess

to Her lips.

# GO MAD WITH ME!

Come!

Read my poetry

and go mad with me

about all the dazzling wonders

this Universe is plotting

on our behalf.


Come!

Read my poetry

and let's eavesdrop together

on those great secrets

shared between the flower's heart

and the sun,

those intimacies

that awaken the closed eyes

of the bud

to the astonishment

of all this great light!

Come!

And let us stop pretending

the stars are a tough crowd

and let's get on with remembering

they're a wild, jovial audience

in nighttime's great arena

applauding and applauding

with their golden hands

our courageous stumble,

our tender, earthly mess,

all those silly, forgivable things

we get up to

down here.


Come!

let us stop this lifeless practice

of enabling each other into forgetting

this world is anything but a jewel-packed

orbed blessing

and that this song of wonderment

some Cosmic Composer

sung into you

is ceaseless.


Come!

Join me

in coming out of denial

that the only thing our hearts

have ever wanted to do

is let down their hair,

loosen up

and admit

that we're surrounded

by nothing

but great wild beauty!


Yes, let us make a firm commitment

to stop enabling

these wild hearts

to do anything but exactly

what they've always wanted to do—


to do anything

but love!

# THE WISE, WILD, HAIRY WOMAN

May we all surrender

to the wise, wild, hairy woman

within ourselves

who represents

the full embrace

of the holy mess,

who doesn't need

to take up space

because she's made of it

while also embodying

the quintessence

of substance.

She breaks bullshit

like rustic bread

She dances cracks

into every system

of fear and facade,


She knows pain is a cauldron

slowly brewing us

into new magic.


Her riches come

from claiming the treasure trove

of stories

within Her wrinkles

and showcasing her collection

through Her broad, abundant smile,


Her heart is a warm home

welcoming all of Herself

and all of you.


She is the host

to the gorgeously undone

who knows tears

water the flowers

in the wild garden

of the heart


She is the alchemist

of all your old attempts

at perfection

allowing the taste

of unforced, authentic gold.


She says to each scrawny

and fragmented

part of ourselves,


"Come, my dear,

there is no virtue

in staying hungry

this world needs you

whole.

Now let's put some fat

on your bones."

# TODAY LET'S BE RICH

Today, let's be rich.

Why not

let the sun name you

the beneficiary

of the great inheritance

of her golden light?


This type of generous wealth

that lights all who notice it

is fine to gloat about.


Today, I wish us the wealth

of increased porousness

of soul

to all things lovely,

that every species of beauty

may flock to you

and you may be a magnet

to meaning.

Today let's be rich with knowing

that we share a world

with the wide collection of beauties

curated into the month of May,


and that the wonders of the world

are mirrors

for the wonders within us.


Let us relax into allowing

any tautness

we carry

to be the tuned strings

for life's music to play upon,


and may the gushing gift

of our existence

rise up within us

like a glorious geyser

of hallelujahs.


May light, like water,

flow into every cracked open space

in you

and may the mouth of your soul

become a gaping hole

for grace.


Today may the sun

be a golden glass

raised all day long

in a cheers with heaven

to your existence


and may the luminous guests of stars

at life's well attended celebration

take over at nighttime.


Today let's be rich

with our noticing

of the detail, texture,

nuance, depth,

richness and satisfaction

of the fine brushstrokes of all things

that the world acquires

upon our awakening to it.


Darling, today may we celebrate

every exquisite moment

of ourselves.

# SOUL DOCTOR

I wasn't feeling well

so I went to the soul doctor.


She looked deeply into

my eyes

and said,

"Ahhh, I see.


I see a brilliant soul in a world

that hasn't yet learned

how to whirl.


Darling, I prescribe you

dancing,

singing,

poetry writing,

the uninhibited sharing

of your every gift.

Drink in this special tincture

of starlight.


Take in a concentrated dose

of beauty

during and between meals.

Put the warm compress

of sunlight

over every part of your body

and know of a certainty

there has only ever been

one You!


And you are an essential nutrient

to all things

and your emergence

is the exact

prescription

for yourself

and the ailing of this world.

Come forward with your light

and heal both."

# YOU TOO CAN AWAKEN LIKE THAT

Breathe the same breath

the trees in the rainforest breathe

that so brings their vibrancy

to life—

you too can awaken

like that.


Cry the same full-skied tears

the clouds cry

that refresh the world

and nurture

the roots of all things

that will one day blossom.


Connect with the electric vitality

of lightning,

catalyze the exhilaration

of your fire

and strike forth

with your mighty

loving force.


Drink in the same sweet light

the cup of each flower

uses as an ablution

to wash her beautiful,

open face


and restore yourself

with reverence

for the answered prayer

of each breath.

# DON'T BE SO TOP DOWN

Don't be so top down
controlling your heart
and your feelings
with your thoughts.

Your heart
is not a wild animal
to be tied and tamed
and yanked around.

Your heart is a Queen.
Your beautiful body,
your wise feelings
her Queendom.

More often than not, your thoughts
would be very, very wise
to respect Her majesty
and bow.

# THE SACRED WEARS A GOOD COSTUME

The sacred wears a good costume.

She loves to dress up

as the ordinary.


Sometimes, like a queen

in peasant clothes

She cloaks herself in the mundane

to get a break

from all that fawning.


So how do you know it's Her

in there?


Look closer at things, when you can,

and to your heart

She'll give a certain

knowing wink.

# THE PERMISSION POEM

I give you permission

to write bad poems,

to sing out of key,

to dance like a clod.


I give you permission

for your heart to have edges,

to be sea glass

not yet fully

sanded smooth,


to love imperfectly

and to let yourself

off the hook for that now and then,

even laugh about it.


I give you permission

to be awkward,

miserable at times, miserly and scared.

to be glorious some days

and wretched many others,

for your life to be

a sacred scribble.

I give you permission

to snuggle up with God now

just as you are

the full package deal

with all your amenities

of sweetness and sin.

I give you full, full permission

to carry on

with the start and stall of humanness

lurching toward spirit

and to know that very few of us,

if any,

have a smooth ride.

What authority do I have

to give such permission?—

None.


This poem is a plagiary

of your own heart.

# HEART WARRIORS

Here's to the heart warriors

who awkwardly, anxiously, timidly

but courageously

do what they can to open that beating fistful

of God every day

and share its beauty.

Here's to those who refuse to stop

bringing forth the balm of their precious light

to the thirsty lips of the world.

Here's to those who believe

our pride can be pulverized

into tenderness

if we keep opening to honesty

and to those who keep working to make diamonds

from that coal.

Here's to those who never stop

believing this world

can be so much more than it is,

who know there is a rose

inside of this bud

and to those who never stop using

their lives to water it.

# IT'S FINALLY HEALED

The sign

that it's finally

healed

is when a wound

is alchemized

into a story

that dresses

the wound

of another.

# INBUILT MEDICINE

If there's something

inside of you

you're still warring with

it just means you haven't yet

fully connected

with the innocence

at its root.


Connection with this sweet

inbuilt medicine

at the base of even

the greatest wound,

that heals and informs

all sorrow

and delivers you

into compassion's soft arms,


is just another way to say

forgiveness.

# OUR GREAT COCOON

Suffering is our great cocoon.

Your budding wings

might not be ready for you

to fully emerge

in your lifetime

But tending to this sacred process

of no longer repressing

or projecting your sorrow

but letting it transform you

as it's intended

is still profoundly noble

and meaningful work.

Stay strong, dear one.

Whether or not you taste the sky

you are building the future

of humanity's wings.

# THE TUNING FORK

Our understandings of God

are malleable—

why not adapt them

until they resonate only

with the tuning fork

of love?

# SPEAK YOUR GREAT DESIRES

Speak your great desires

especially if you think them childish

and unattainable,


Especially if you struggle

with self-worth

and have for too long

been holding your joy

hostage.


Speak your great desires

that you think might be

completely impractical

and that you doubt will make you

much money.


Speak your great desires

whose wings are almost too precious

to give to the sky

knowing its the risk our soul's must take

to unfurl ourselves

for the chance of flight.


Speak your great desires

if they have loose threads

and aren't fully

put together—


put your love before

your perfectionism!


Speak your great desires—

the outcome

is secondary.


The goal is for your light

that nourishes the entire Universe

to be offered forth

as a great honor

to yourself.

# THERE IS A LIGHT WITHIN YOU

There is a light

that is always within you—

you cannot be truly rejected.


There is a light

that is always within you

that the Universe warms Herself on—

you can never be truly alone.


You are made from the Essence

of the breath of life—

what bad salesman

has convinced you

that death could be real?


As we un-spin ourselves

from illusion

we find everything we've always sought

has always been

twinkling from within—

the richness

of the Universe

like a coy little secret

in our chests


and bit by bit we discover

there was never

any shortage

of God.

# LET US DANCE!

Can the old, dying God

inside of you survive?

No.

Not unless He's willing

to be revitalized

by the Goddess within,

Not unless He allows

that tender, mighty touch

to give His breathless soul

mouth to mouth

resuscitation

and let Her vital life-force

of open hearted courage,

of vulnerable longing,

of grieving surrender,

of deep, deep beauty,

of connection

fully back in,


Not unless He becomes willing

to let the verses of Her poetry

rewrite His old stories

and put some dance

in the doctrine ,


Not unless he becomes willing

to let the straight and narrow merge

with with the wide and winding


and make the needle's eye

considerably more accommodating


Not unless He allows

His Wild Woman within

to let down Her hair

and decode His heart

with those wild locks,

Not unless He lets Her

take up so much space

inside of Him

He can finally breathe

and relax.

Yes, the old, dying God

in humanity's chest

needs emergency treatment,

that Kiss of Life

that comes from admitting

deep frailty,

and the restoration

of finally

falling to our knees

to receive help.

For Father God to gather

His true strength,

He must bow before the Her

He's tucked away in Himself

and finally nourished

stand again with a new fullness—


God and Goddess

reborn as equals

through humanity's deep breath


and in astonishment of the other

reach out a hand

to close the ancient distance

and weeping and rejoicing say:


"At last!

Let us dance"

# THE GREAT MOTHER

The Great Mother

has beautiful intentions

for this earth

that She's set in motion.


She has set in motion

the blossoming of a great sisterhood

in which all women world wide

join hands and hearts

like a garland of roses.


She has set in motion

for the many religions

to be strung together like prayer beads

that the many names of God

may be chanted together

in one glorious song,

and for the various hues of skin

and different tones of culture

to be a great source of celebration—


for our world's divine, delectable diversity

to be our earth's great prize,


for us to prance through our lives

like delighted flower girls

sprinkling our petaled blessings

with each step,


and for each life to be a celebration

between our hearts

and whatever they should encounter

of the great wedding

of love to love,


and for each thought and word and movement

to renew our vows.

Yes, our world is Her gorgeous prayer,

Her precious seed,

full of luminous potential

that She's planted

in the luscious, fertile darkness

of our Universe


while continually watering it

with light.


Our realization

of Her great intentions

is its bloom.

# SO THIRSTY

When you see beauty

in another

or in yourself

you shine light upon it—

this is how we grow

toward blossom.

Oh it's a fool's errand

to repress the sunshine

in your chest

whose nature is to shine forth

and water each other

with our generous witnessing.

.

Withhold not, dear one.

The world of the heart

is so thirsty to flower

into a radiant star.

# LET'S BOIL IT DOWN

There's a desire

built deep within us

to be one

with every human heart

we encounter,

to feel every part

of this earth

and our equally soft and sweet

and beautiful bodies

as the warmest,

most secure and loving homes,

and to relate

to The Great Creator

of this extraordinary nest

for our development

as the most Hospitable,

Caring Host

It's time for the shy queens and kings

within us

to be reticent with our nobility

no more

and take the throne of our hearts

to rule with unabashed love.

Dear one,

let's boil it down:

if there's profound grief

you carry inside of you

it's because we're still

so far from this.

If there's beautiful desire

for change

within you

it's to bring us all together

closer to this.

# SOPPING

God loves to repose

into every atom of this world,

including your body,

and drench it with light.


When I hear people talk

about their loneliness or limitations

I often want to shout,


"Darling, can't you see

every part of you

is sopping with God!?"

# THE JONESES

The Joneses

gathered the neighbors around them

to finally let them in

on the messy, endearing, humanizing

truth

in their own hearts:


"Enough with the act, y'all,

let's get real.

You gotta stop trying

to 'keep up with us'

we can barely keep up

with ourselves!


It's all looked put together

on the outside

but on the inside

our minds are un-mowed lawns,

our inner child

is a drop out,

our nervous system

is full of weeds and chipped paint,

we haven't taken the trash out

of our childhood conditioning

for years!


And it's really starting

to build up.


This world—

our big neighborhood—

could use a good, long break

from facade.


So what say we all cut the B.S.

and just try to 'keep up'

with accepting

every bit of ourselves

as our worthy, messy hearts

do their stumbling best?

# BLOOMING IS CONTAGIOUS

Blooming is contagious,

the whole hillside

gets infected

come the colorful pandemic

of springtime,


it goes around quick:


some ring leader

gets this wild idea

to risk everything it's known

for the sake

of unforeseen color

that a wild tenderness

might emerge


and the ecstatic message

of the flower's openness says

to the not yet opened buds,

"It's in you too!"


Oh, cozy up

to people like this

who make you think,


"There might be something

exquisitely wonderful

inside of me

that's susceptible

to sunshine

and damnit,

I'm gonna do whatever it takes

to figure out what!"

# UNFOLDING PRAYER

Every stage of the flower

is an expression of enlightenment:


The seed

has completely arrived

full of glee

at its potential


Its cracking open

is a great exaltation

as it's dismantled into everything

it might become.


What amazement

experiences the sprout

to be the experience

of new life

shooting out of its own body!

The bud is a full-bodied

burgeoning prayer,

the silent reverence

before blossom.


And finally, the bloom,

when it meets face to face

with its Beloved,

sunlight.


Darling, there is no part of your process

from tight, hard seed

to full-petaled blossom

that isn't deeply sacred,


Drink in every part of yourself—

you are The Beloved's

unfolding prayer.

# DO PRAY

Whether or not
the concept of God
supports you,
do pray

Prayer gives voice
to your heart
and mobilizes your desires

Everything in this Universe
is energetically linked,
and like an invisible root system,
information and resources
are shared,

and words are the ambassadors
of what we think and feel
to the Universe's Great Ears
that exist everywhere.

The sun and the bud

have the same yearning

to bring the inner essence

of the rose forward.


Trust that the precious desires

already folded into you,

petal-like,

are placed there to blossom.

What if your truest, sweetest desires

and that of The Great Wild Beloved

might just be one?


If this theory even might be true

that there's something generous and receptive

about this Universe

and that channels open

when we ask them to...


well, any good scientist

would be wise

to experiment.

# TEND TO BOTH

Suffering blossoms

into compassion,

grief waters tenderness.


Your light and shadows

are an ecosystem

intricately connected

into one another

sharing nutrients

like love notes

between roots.


Tend to both—

this is how we grow.

# THERE'S AN ESSENCE

There's an Essence

within you

that can neither be

enhanced

nor diminished.


It spans Universes

and embraces the minuscule,

the infinitesimal.


It is infinite

in the way that the numbers

between 0 and 1

are infinite

which is complete

and wondrously,

eternally satisfying,


and yet allows for infinitely more infinities.

It is the exaltation of the hermit crab

when it ceases to need

to scurry from shell to shell

to find respite.


This Essence dips into pools

of intergalactic radiance

for play and restoration,

it tickles the stars

and high fives

the suns.


It has no need to bypass

the trappings

of the small mind

but nor does it take them too seriously.


There is nothing to prove or do or please

to earn this—

this is your birthright


that I solemnly swear

no—joyfully exclaim!

all humanity is growing into.

# THE KISS

Bring the kiss

of your consciousness


to the forehead of each wound

and exclaim,


"Thank you, gift!

What gems you have

within you!"

# I'M HERE TO ROCK YOUR SMALL BOAT

I'm here to rock

your small boat

and knock you into the sea.


Believe it or not

this kind of capsizing

is what we've all been praying for


because you never were meant

to be that small,

unstable boat—

you have always been the sea.


I no longer feel

like enabling you away

from drowning every illusion

in your great vastness,


I am ready to introduce you

to your power,

for every pore of your knowing

to drink in

its profound depths.

# THE SKY PROPOSED TO ME

The sky proposed

to me tonight

in star diamonds.


This happens each night, of course

to any heart who will notice it.


Sometimes we miss the moves

the beauty of this Universe

is always trying to put on us.


Sometimes we need a poem

to properly translate

Her great love language,


to properly unpack

all the gifts

the world is always trying

to lay at our feet,

This poem has offered

to be such a side-kick

and nudge you under the table

in hopes that you might finally

take a hint.

# CRUSHED INTO WINE

To the God

who does not make

all of us famous,

to She who is not

an enabler

of the great dreams of the grapes

that instead they may be crushed

into wine.

To She who does not want to grant

the coal

deliverance from its suffering

just yet,

for somehow She sees within it

the makings

of unimaginable diamonds.

To She who does not respond

to the caterpillar's prayers

to be all that it can be

and instead makes it devour itself

to bring forth the latent wings

it never would have known.


To She who impoverishes

every illusion

we thought was so precious.


To She who is so happy to dash

any fantasy we've had of ourselves,

to prove our inner riches and nobility

more magnificent and abundant

than anything the external

could ever have crowned us with.


To She who steals

every smallness

I hang my name on—

thank You,

from who I will become.

# UNFLINCHING LIGHT

Set your feet squarely.

Look the world directly

in the eye

and become fully visible

Yes, this power is rare,

to bring your heart forward

like the precious gem that it is,

knowing the world

might not yet have grown

the capacity

to properly witness

such unflinching light—

it requires a specialized courage

that you were made for.

Fear not your exposure.

What will be revealed

in your great willingness

to emerge from ancient hiding

is the precise encouragement

our deep souls all so need

to roll the boulders of illusion

out of light's way.

# LET YOUR LIGHT POUR

Call your dear ones

right now

and tell them

how exquisite they are.


In the business and hubbub of things

we can forget to pause

and let the collection

of our life's gratitude flock

to us.


In our haste

we can outpace

the still pools

of presence in our hearts

so desiring to gather

all our precious ones into it

and behold their magnificence,

and isn't to miss that

truly the only

great tragedy?


Today, put one thing

on your to-do list:

to let your light pour

generously upon all things

you have loved.

# RASCALLY DAY

There are some

precious nights

when my perspective

is screwed on right

when I snuggle in

between my two small kids

sleeping and warm

and sweet as can be


and I think,

"I created the loves of my life."


And I know God feels this way

as She too snuggles in to our hearts

each night

so beyond satisfied, content

and adoring of Her work...

even after our very

rascally day.

# WE CAN BE THAT VAST

No more squeezing your light

into small spaces.


No more cutting down

your truth.


No more pretending yourself

a drop

holding the seas

of your power

at bay.


No more of this being

a marionette to society's trappings,

letting them move you

at their diminishing whims.


No more pretending

you're not a spiritual essence

full of Divine majesty and mystery.

No more dressing your beauty down
to fit this world—

emerge a cascade of magnificent light!

I collected all the sweet stars
into my chest tonight—

darling, don't you know
we can be that vast?

Yes, the great magnitude
of our love is what the Universe
is expanding into.

✤

# MORE THAN MYSTICAL

More than mystical,

my poetry is human.


At times

God passes me a beauty code

to be written down

and passed from heart

to heart

to unlock

the world.


At other times

my poetry licks its fingers

after finishing a bag of potato chips

all by itself

and reclines on the couch

to talk about the importance

of embracing our wholeness—

bags of potato chips, Divine Essence

and all.

At times my poetry is rage

and wants nothing more

than to decapitate light

hungry for spaciousness

and the wider embrace

that only the darkness can offer.


At times my poetry is so small

and beseeches anything

that can remind her

of greater connection.


And while yes,

on occasion the ideal self

does pop in

to guide, love, inform

and laugh with the rest,


rather than transcend it,

it knows its only purpose

is to feed the full

authentic self.


My poetry will decline

the dehumanization

of expectation

to stay "mystical."


It wants to wear no robes,

wants to come home

in a cozy way

rather than further exile

into the barren lands of image

and facade,


and desires most

to release itself from fragmented

versions of self

on its path toward the full breath

of wholeness.

The soul that writes this poetry

would rather relax honestly

into the all of it

than force itself to balance

high up

on a tight wire

of light.


My poetry has many faces

some of them marvelously ordinary

and she would like all of them

to beam forth,

supremely unveiled.

# NO WAY OUT OF GOD

The thesis statement

of most all my poetry

is

that you really don't need a promotion

in this great, wild life

to be deemed worthy.


You came here with 5 stars

attached to your every movement

and word and breath.


The cosmos are in ceaseless applause

of your existence at all


and if you get quiet enough

you can hear

this wild celebration

of light.

Even every wound

is an entryway,

not an error


and try as you might

there is no way out

of God.

# NO MORE SPIRITUAL ARROGANCE

No more spiritual arrogance,

please.


Sure, your meditation practice

is good


but every person on this earth

goes into the deepest meditation

for about eight hours

every night.


Every person is born enlightened

if that means bewildered with love and awe—

which seems a good definition—


so if you think yourself closer to that

than some adults

you're still probably farther from it

than most babies

The blueberry bush,

so delighted to share

the fruits of its life

so generously with any hand,

is the best candidate for a guru


and the sweetness your whole ambitious life

is searching for

is spilling out

of the simplest moments.


Everyone is a mystic

who keeps trying their fumbling best

to open their heart now and then


and a mystical poet

is nothing more than someone

who lets all the beauty and wisdom

wrapped up in an ordinary flower

elbow them now and then

and tell them to take a hint.

Speaking of the ordinary,

that's God's favorite place

to hang out,


and a great practice

for sound mental health

is found in balancing

the right and left hemispheres

of your brain


with your hands working together

while doing a big load

of dishes

or making some simple bread.


Darling, bottom line, we're all beautifully

animated dust

and to make any kind of hierarchy

comparing dust to dust

seems rather silly,

does it not?

# PROBING JOY

I can't keep quiet

when there are still so many hearts

that need resuscitation,

so much buried power and truth,

so many gifts

to be resurrected!


The richness waiting in you to be tapped

is the inspired ink

into which I dip

my pen.


Like a scientist

who cannot stop penetrating

new frontiers of this Universe


My pen cannot stop

probing the farthest reaches

of joy

to prove again and again

there are countless dimensions

of you

yet to be discovered!

I cannot stop revealing the evidence

that within every darkness

can be found Universes

of whirling light!

# THIS WORLD WHERE BEES DANCE

We did not come to this world,

where bees dance

to tell each other

where the nectar is,

to walk in a straight line.


We did not come to this world,

in which the whole purse

of stars has been poured out

into the deep wishing well

of the night

that by their light

all things may come to life,

to deprive ourselves

of blossom.


We did not come to this world,

in which flowers

crack themselves open

entirely undoing their hiding

with the greater impulse

to share their beauty,

to conform to tight rules

that keep us safe

and unexposed


We did not come to this world,

in which seeds become towering trees

and the Universe gleefully expands

into Her own mystery,

to play small


We did not come to this world,

every bit of which

is so wild with desire

to bring forth its love,

for our hearts

to stay tame.

# DEEP LIGHT

This world is hungry

for a deep light

that can only be harvested

through our shadows.


Our souls are hungry

for a spirituality

that allows

the full range of our authentic being,

that doesn't insist on our shallow light

while cutting the depths

of our darkness off

at the knees.


Our hearts are hungry

for a feeling of home

that allows all of us back in

even and especially

our most exiled and condemned parts,

our most lawless and impoverished

and impossible to control parts,

our most disheveled, unkempt

parts

that have never known


how to put themselves together

or how to gloss on a false smile.


Our hearts are screaming

for these parts of us

to return


with that kind of desperate love

of a mother

separated from her child


and our shadows

are equally vulnerable and quaking

with desperate desire

to be summoned home.

# THE CANDLES OF OURSELVES

We are here

to bring forth our light

and hold the candles

of ourselves

to each other.

# A QUICKER ROUTE

We've been taught

to think of God

as being supremely disciplined,

a master of morality,

and keeping commitments—

the truth is

She'll throw it all out

again and again

each time She finds a quicker route

to get to your heart.

# TRUE SPIRITUALITY VOTES

True spirituality

is not another fragmented way

that makes us look good

but doesn't change

our hearts.


True spirituality

must comprehensively

address and support

all areas of life—


emotional and psychological health

and social justice,


these areas must not

be left out and ignored.


True spirituality breathes

God into the darkest shadow

that the heart may weep out

all those pains it took in

and believed about itself

that were never true.


Social justice is part and parcel

of true spirituality.


True spirituality votes.


True spirituality must sensitize the heart

to its own suffering

that it may be unable to tolerate or bear

that of another.


True spirituality

doesn't transcend

as an abandonment of ourselves and the world

but rather brings us fully into it.


True spirituality

is rarely comfortable

it is co-creating with God a cocoon

for all your illusions


and agreeing to be destroyed

to be transformed—


and spoiler alert:

this terrible, necessary process

does not only happen once.


True spirituality is messy.

It introduces you

to all your shortcomings

that they may not be fixed

but held and kissed.


It's becoming a shadow Sherpa

familiarizing you with the dark

that you may be released

from fear and judgment of it.

True spirituality

is embodied.

All those concepts

that made you look so good in public

will have to be thrown out


that you may go through the gnarly gauntlet

of learning how to be truly kind

to those in your own home


and to yourself

when you meet you own eyes in a mirror.


True spirituality wants you

to strip yourself of every old ideology

that has led you to harming anything


and breathe love

into your full belly

giving an extra dose

to all those love deprived places

you used to call your enemies.

# DRINK IN THE STARS

Ladies,

the only thing I want us to change

about our bodies

is the way we seem them—


the Goddess has been hitching a ride

in our hips

since the beginning,


there are seas hidden in you,

moons of wisdom

in your womb,


your line of ancestors

sings up your spine,


the secrets of the cosmos

are folded into every part

of your softness.

As women we were born

with the unshakable birthright


to set both feet squarely

on the firm, solid ground

of our worth

that's always been waiting

to hold us.


It's time to disown these small myths

that we are not the sacred love child

of the sea and the moon,


it's time to reclaim

and pour holy oil on

the brilliance in our souls

that was never meant

to be dimmed,


it's time to reclaim

the power of our softness

Darling, it's time to get us fed.

Now let's fling open the oceans

in our hearts

and drink in the stars.

# THE WILD RUMPUS OF THE ANCESTORS

Once you start to heal

all that old pain

you came in with

the ancestors start

yipping and hollering

through your chest,

"now go fulfill your great desires!"

# GOD BRINGS ME CLOSE

Some days God brings me close

and in those moments

all those places in me

that have believed themselves to be so unworthy

must pause

as love rushes in to fill all the gaps.

I contemplate

what a gift

to be a participant

in this world

of texture, color, light

and what an extraordinary gift

to be able to love

anything at all.

# NO PATH TO GOD

There is no "path"

to God,

no paved road,

no one way.

God is a wild land,

an infinitely directional landscape.

Each world is a dew drop

in one of Her rose gardens

that so effortlessly

and intentionally contains

all of your worst deeds

Each multiverse

is one of Her most contented

sighs.

Talk like this can make people crazy—

"you mean...there's no way out

of this love?!


Then what of our most precious illusions

of good and bad?


How will I continue to judge people

if God is so soluble

in everything?!"


Binaries wilt here—

darling, there's only a process

of waking up

to Her endless embrace


When we approach

this circumference-less love


all of those ancient civilizations

within us

made with the bricks of self-hatred, self-judgment

right and wrong, saved and damned

fall to their knees

and cry,


"ooooh, ohhhh, ohhhh!"

# ADVERTISEMENT FOR JOY

This life wants you
to be its walking advertisement
for joy.

To blare this message
loud and proud
and also with nuance

filled with the fine print
of peace and inner delight,

and the subliminal messaging
of acceptance and wholeness
written into every movement—

the lift of your smile,
the way your glance
falls upon things,
whatever your heart

rushes towards,

your bravery at finally

pursuing those things

that have always called you,

the wink in your soul.


Oh, let life use you this way

to be its finest marketing rep


to sway masses

towards their hearts.


It doesn't promise to pay

but I promise


this job was made

for you.

# WILDFIRE

A wildfire came through me today.

It seemed, at first, a crisis

all those precious forests burned down

that took so long to grow

so many precious structures

dashed

until I remembered

it's only the belief of lack

in the organism's ability

to regrow

that causes stress

when things break down,

only the fear that things cannot heal

which makes us overprotect ourselves

at the fear of a wound.

Rooted beneath the charred surface

is so much pulsing vitality, untouched.


so much unalterable, irrepressible,

growth, healing, renewing


L I F E.


As sacred as those forests are,

as cherished as all those old structures were,

its the life within them that makes them so


and that life is ever abiding

and there is plenty of it,

in fact, it breathes through me now,


"Ahhhhhhhh..."

# FALSE NAMES FOR GOD

Of all the false names

you have for God

start by throwing out "Judge."


God has no podium,

no gavel.


She longs to celebrate you,

to sing to you,

to kiss you awake.


The only structure She yearns for

is that which will support

your growing happiness,


more a trellis

than a set of hard laws.


Divine punishment isn't real

it's an illusion with sharp claws.


Sin means

not drinking in as much light

as you possibly could have.


The straight and narrow?

This life is an ever widening unfoldment

of your luminosity!


Do I still need to tell you

to throw out the strict,

authoritarian binary

of heaven and hell?


Can we at last step outside the bounds

of the linear march toward salvation

and begin to see God

dancing spirals

throughout all creation?


If you get quiet and hold God

to your heart

like a shell to your ear

to hear Her whispers more vast

than the sea,


don't you already know

everything this poem is telling you?


Have we ever wanted anything but God

to be an open heart

to fall fully into?

# VOWS TO BEAUTY

I no longer want

to hurt in private.


I no longer want

to keep God at arm's length.


I want to stop the harsh demands

that I clean myself up first

and just allow love

to flood

my broken heart.


I want to stop turning down

the stars proposals

to marry me

and stop resisting the persistent,

generous suitors

God has placed within all life.

Oh, I'm ready,

to make and keep

my vows to beauty.


I'm ready for the pangs

of closeness.


I did not come to this earth

to be a mere acquaintance

of love.

# YANK THAT CORK

I was a bottle of champagne

waiting quietly

in God's cellar,

effervescence held in,

keeping it to myself.

But today, God decided

to choose me

and yank that cork.

Darling, your only prayer

needs to be this:

"God I'm ready for you

to celebrate existence

through me

and dear God

I'd like to get this party started

N O W."

# HOW BEAUTIFUL THAT IS

What can great poetry do?

All a great poem can hope to do

is validate what your deep heart

already knows

and show you how beautiful

that is.

# THE SCENT OF YOUR BEAUTY

I have been so cruel

I can now forgive

most all cruelty in you.


I have seen such profound

helplessness and insecurity

inside myself

I can now easily find the dignity

within yours too.


I've rent so many veils asunder

suffocated with illusion

as I was

I now have something of x-ray vision—


darling, there is little in you anymore

that can convince me away from your light.


I've come to see your shadows

as the poorest salesmen

trying to sell you off

for something so much less

than you so clearly are.


I have touched profound beauty and truth

beneath each false self.


Now there is almost no act

you can perform,

no heckling phantom

that can throw me off


the scent of your beauty.

# HER SACRED, RECKLESS THING

Dear one,

we are all here on this earth

for the great work of love

and love is not

for the faint of heart.


If you are on this earth

you are a tall, mighty tree

inside of a small seed—

love is what breaks you open.


Love is the systematic destroyer

of every small self.


She is the unruly one.


She is what germinates

the inside of heartbreak

Love is the only true
evolutionary force in this Universe—
the only thing we desire enough
to make us grow
beyond ourselves.


Love is the only thing persuasive enough
to convince us to take on that harrowing voyage
from bud to blossom.


And all that said,


I hope you can let her in
to do her sacred, reckless, living thing
to the heart of your life anyway.

# GOD IS A HOARDER

God is a bit of hoarder, really,

when it comes to love and beauty.

Have you taken a good, hard look

at Her living room,

this earth?

It's packed to the gills!

Beauty stacked from floor to ceiling—

you really can't go anywhere here

without stepping on one of Her trinkets.

And there's no stopping Her—

She keeps collecting more stars,

gets a whole new order

of springtime

each year.

Darling, the point of this quirky poem

is to remind you that there's no need

to be a minimalist with love here.


In fact, perhaps it's time to stop this practice

of being so allergic

to having more than enough.


You should probably be warned though,

if you're overwhelmed by Her great stockpile

of goodness out there,


before opening to Her greatest stash

inside the closet doors

of your heart.

# SACRED EXPERIMENT

Today will you join me

in a sacred experiment?


Just for today, let's stop pretending

that love is a snob

for whom we'll never be good enough.


Today, let's gift ourselves

the dark chocolate

of our shadows.


Let's bring love down

from the mountain top

to flood our lowlands too.


Let's cease making love a ravishing,

lofty destination

and bring her down to earth

to let her join us

in each ordinary step.


Today can we decide our imperfect heart

is worthy of love

right now, just as it is

without dressing up?


What if love desires more of a collapse

than a straight spine,

more of a willingness to stumble

than a perfect step?

What if she's offering

her hand to you now

before you've even learned the dance?


Darling, let's stop perfecting our grapes

and today allow our acceptance

to surrender us into wine.


Yes, just for today,

let's just see how all that goes.

# WE ARE THE MYTH MAKERS

We are the myth makers,

our lives are pens

writing with our movements, our steps,

our actions, every touch

the stories we're hoping to record

into the world.


What are the styles of relating

we hope to inscribe?


What is the tone

of our presence here

as we walk this soft earth?


Women, what stories

would we like to tell

about our selves,

about our sisterhood,

about our strength?

Men, what stories would you

like to tell

about gentleness and power

coexisting,

about the great courage

it takes to love?


Humanity what stories

do we want to tell


about the grand journey

to finally opening our hearts

to each other?


Darling, it's time to put

our heads together

and consider:


how beautiful

dare we make

this world?

# TINDER PROFILE IN THE AGE OF FEMINISM

I will roar so loudly

it will wake your most deeply

sleeping dragons,

you may not project their fire

onto me,

you must let it burn through

every old way.


I don't enable smallness,

I want

to take up space.


My words can dismantle

every old god, hierarchy and entitlement

and cast them aside.


I want to bring you

not to your knees

but into your hips,

that birthplace of creation,

where we may remake

the old definitions

for men, women, relating.


I want to take

the corset off of nighttime,

let every shadow breathe.


My words are a sword,

they will pull you forth

from the legacy

of your truth's every sheathed blade.


My presence will pluck

preciously held lies

off of you

like leeches you'd thought

to be embedded jewels.


Not having first been

utterly destroyed

by the kiss

of your Inner Goddess

is a red flag for me.


Forget all your good lines,

I only listen to circles.


Of course there will be

no eyelash batting,

my hips have high standards,

my lips are spitfire truths.


I'm more raw than fresh kale

and often, I sneer.


Oh...and I like Italian food.

# RECOVERY PROGRAM

My name is Chelan Harkin

and I am in the ongoing recovery program

from the addiction

to the paradigms of the past.


I'm trying to become

sober from facade,

a renunciate of half-truths,

a teetotaler of pretense.


It's time to transform our hearts

and this world

with our truth

one day at a time.

# TELL ME MORE!

The sun says,

"Tell me more! Tell me more!"

to the flower's heart.


What else would make it blossom?


Love invites the sweetest parts

of us forward and dear one,

I've heard the same invitation

from an even warmer, greater source

of light


calling so lovingly and curiously

to every bud in your soul,


"Darling, tell me more!"

# FOLLOW YOUR SWEET DESIRES

The flower benefits

from the hummingbird

following her sweet desire

for nectar.


Darling, it's the same for us—

all hearts will be pollinated

by you

following the honeyed river

of your soul's desires.

# YOU WERE VERY BRAVE

You were very brave

to have come to a place

where your light

would not always be seen.


Often it feels like we've signed

a strict, invisible contract

with each other

agreeing to keep this great light,

this truth inside of us,

tucked away

and held back.


But you've felt the stirrings,

haven't you?,

of knowing

all this hiding

must soon end?

It seems to me

the end of times

is rumbling

within our hips, our ribs,

our voices


this great light readying itself

to emerge


knowing once it comes out

it can never be put back away for good

again.

# YOU MUST FEED IT THIS

Like the trees and the leaves,

our souls are photosynthetic

though not to physical light


but, oh, they are porous

to music, poetry, beauty


in fact they need these kinds

of square meals to survive.


If you want your life

to bear sweet fruit


you must feed it

this.

# A MORE LOVING CANDIDATE

As you're recovering

from the old, dying god

we've inherited

from our forefathers

that hasn't served you,

as we all are,


and the boss of your heart

has finally gained the courage

to be open to hire

a more loving candidate

for Lord of The Universe—

this time around

it's time to get

some standards:


This time, make sure God

feel like a close sister

holding you on your worst days.

Insist that God be big enough

for the full range of your collapse.


Tell this God

She must be available

to buoy your joy.


You're tired of being shamed

and gas-lit

by the Creator,

creating us imperfect

and then blaming us for it.


Tell Her you've long deserved something better.

You want Her to be as attentive

as each breath,


you want Her to be your watering hole,

a place where your soul

can reliably drink.

No more hiding your heart

and tiptoeing

around some myth

of Her wrath .


Let it be known

you're no longer afraid

to hurt God's feelings

with your truth,

and quite frankly,

the fragile/abusive old god paradigm

could stand to grow

in resilience.


Announce that you're tired

of being a martyr

and ready to pull life close

to tell it exactly what you want.


It's time to set some boundaries:

Tell Her you're not looking for a rebound

and if She doesn't have the qualifications

you're looking for

you'll settle for celestial anarchy


until you until you find

the right fit.

# SO FEWER WORDS

We could really get by

with so fewer words—

"Hallelujah!"

would be almost enough

or its secular version,

"Wow!"

The cowboy rendition,

"Yeehaw!"

would work

or just an,

"Ahhhhhhh"

from a satisfied heart.

We could probably get by

just fine on

"Om,

Shalom,

Assalamualaikum."

Yes, perhaps a word fast,

which in reality would be a word feast,

is in order—

words that roll the Universe

around in our mouths,

that allow us to feel

Her curves

dancing meaning

to the world

off the stage of our tongues,

that let us taste

the AWE

inside of G-AWE-D.

When we boil down language

it seems the only sounds we really need

and all we can ever hope to communicate

are those onomatopoeias

that mimic the ecstatic joy

of the in breath

and the out breath

of the soul.

# TOTALLY OVERBEARING

You don't feel loved?!

You must not have yet realized

that God is like the most

cloying, over-the-top

parent.


The angels have become

so bored

about God gushing about you,

going on and on

about how you did

the tiniest little thing

to open your heart,


about how blown away God was

by your infinitesimal new,

brave act.


"He did his first almost loving thing today!"

God announces proudly

of His precious little people

who have just taken their heart's

first step.


"I've gotta write in my journal

about how she considered

telling the truth today—I mean,

she actually almost did it!"


It's really no wonder

you juke away

from God's grace

and spend lifetimes hiding from this love—


God is thiiiiis close

to being totally

overbearing.

# SO MANY WEDDINGS

There were so many weddings

in the chapel of my body last night

I lost count of how many—

my chest felt like Vegas!


The vows here are simple:

when you release the two wild lovers

of all your polarities

in a holy breath of allowance


both sides come rushing in

to each other's arms

in the greatest romance

of dissolving

in the One.

# HOLY NUISANCE

I asked Hafiz

for inspiration

and he poured gasoline

all over my poetry

and set it on fire!


Then he spent the whole night

fanning its flame with his dancing.


He turned the stars into cymbals

and has spent night after night

making quite the golden racket

clanging them together.


When I groaned,

"Hafiz, quiet down—I'm trying to sleep!"

He replied, "This cosmic applause for God

knows no cease!"

He's unleashed muse after muse,

they're buzzing around my consciousness

like mosquitoes

there are so many

sometimes I have to swat one away

before it bites my heart.


Truly, in some moments

it all feels like quite the holy nuisance

but the real truth is

I never, never want this madness

to stop.

# Q AND A WITH HAFIZ

Q: "Hafiz, how do we release ourselves from excessive

attachments to another?"

A: "So far I've only found

one way.

It's to know that whatever

wild obsessions

you're carrying on with about the other,

whatever love songs you just can't stop singing,

however certain you are that your names must be scrawled

together in the stars—

know that God feels exactly the same way

about you.

He even likes to write your last name after His

and pretend

you're married."

✤

# DIVINE RECIPE

The ingredients

for being created

in God's image are:


Deep groove in the hips,

deep laughter in the belly,

an utterly undoing

love

in the heart.


Don't deprive yourself

of Godliness—

Dance!

Laugh!

And be utterly

undone.

# TO APPLAUD YOUR RADIANCE

Really, the whole point of healing

is that it takes less and less work

to be astonished.


You stop demanding

that the world knocks you sideways

and just let the sweetness

of simple things

climb into your heart.


The purpose of healing

is that it takes less and less work

to feel a deep belonging.


The inclusive congregation

of stars,

whose only doctrine is "shine!",

so wants your heart

as a member,

and the community of hillside daisies

considers you as an integral part.


Really, the whole point of healing

is to make an easier time

of love,


that it stop being singled out

as a limited resource,


that you may find your soul mate

winking out at you

through every bit of life ,


and that you remember

each night the moon

sets her light in the sky

to encourage and applaud

your radiance.

# HIDE AND SEEK CHAMPION

God is the great

hide and seek champion.


He likes to play

in the dark

and His favorite hiding spot

is just on the other side

of your deepest heartache.


You've been playing this game for lifetimes

without Him being found—

it's getting a bit old.


Perhaps it's time to look

in that long neglected room

of your great sorrow

and see God's face

pop out

announcing, almost smugly,

"What took you so long? I've been waiting in here
all along!"

# GOOD MEDICINE

There are social conventions

that desperately need to be destroyed

by whatever truth is in your heart.


The specific flavor of magic tonic

that is kept hidden in your chest

is EXACTLY

the medicine this world needs.


It's time to bring it forth!

We are all healers and creators

by being our truest selves.


You, my dear,

are good medicine

and you have been prescribed

to this time.

# WOMEN

Women, we have always been

too big for the patriarchy

We are the rivers

to its damns—

even if we've been trained

to be quiet and timid

there's great, rushing power

within us

No matter the chainsaws

we are the forest

and there is simply no way

to keep Mother Nature

from growing back

again and again and again.

We are the sea,

the small boats

represent the conditioning

that ludicrously claims

it can contain us.


We've heard the demands

that the moon must stay crescent—

we are her great rebellion

of fullness

and her delight

in taking up space.


We've never been

"too sensitive"

we are frontierswomen of feeling

and sensitivity is where

our power lives

perhaps we've simply been

too powerful

for all the small models of thought

that have feebly tried to diminish us.

We are the wild

beneath every

tame trapping,


Our souls are sleeping dragons

made to awaken

to their full power

and the dawn is fast approaching.


We are the roaring thunder

just beneath the thin layer

of fake blue sky we've been taught

we must wear

like a veil

to cover our great and necessary storms.


We are the greatness

stuffed like a Universe

into a small space

before The Big Bang

explodes Her force

into power and life.

We are wild, active volcanoes

in spite of the futile demands

we stay latent.


You can see why

it takes the hyper vigilant effort

of every system

to pretend they're keeping

us down.


We are the irrepressible wholeness

humanity is growing into,


We are where evolution

is going.

# GOD'S MULE

Each poem

tries to smuggle a bundle of God

into your heart.


If it's good,

tucked away just right,

the security officers in your mind

won't catch it.


If they do, they might try to send it back—

"This stuff will mess up our rules

and our sense of order!" they outcry.


They'll make a great fuss

and have this light confiscated

and quarantined

to the small box of their judgments.


I used to hold back,

scared of being sniffed out,

but now I deal to anyone

even remotely interested

in the sweetest, sweetest hit

of the remembrance

of Home.

# USELESS UMBRELLAS

The hardest work

we'll ever do

is holding up

these useless umbrellas

to block ourselves

from all this Grace!

# LOVE PREDICAMENT

As I fall

quite deeply in love

with anyone who has the courage

to have a wide open heart

it makes me think

this whole world

might find itself

in quite a great love predicament

as the masses

wake up.

# THE SACRED COLLAPSE

We're in a season of wailing,

joy will have its time.


First, let's take care

of this tremendous grief

that's been held

in humanity's chest

since time immemorial.


First, let's steward the aching,

the neglected,

the desolate shadows

so longing for a tender touch.


We need to till the dark soil.

Demanding roses of ourselves

before this process

has had its place

is unrealistic

Darling, relax

into your blessed falling.


The sacred collapse

precedes the flowering.

# SATURATED WITH JOY

May your

great ambition be

to alchemize

any ordinary moment

into pure gold

by saturating it

with your joy.

# THE VOID

I strode into the void tonight

to learn

THE BEST NEWS EVER:

The void, it seems, is not the void!

But the darkest, richest

most fertile soil

from whence all light

grows.

# LET US DANCE

Your smarts, your talents, your good looks—

take off these impediments

and let us dance!

# ABOUT THE AUTHOR

Chelan Harkin has been channeling ecstatic poetry for years. The predecessor to this book is *Susceptible to Light* which began her publishing journey and was published only seven months prior to Let Us Dance! Her publishing journey has been mystical and transformational and filled with "prayer experiments" gone right.

Chelan is regularly compared to the great mystic poets, Rumi, Hafiz and Rilke which puts a big grin on her soul.

She is 32 years old and lives in a geographically spectacular region of Washington State, The Columbia Gorge, with her honey sweet husband, Noah, and their two small children. In her poetry and in her life, Chelan continually invites the fumbling, suffering parts of our nature and our divinity to meet for tea in the heart, to have a great laugh and share a big hug.

She feels immense love for her readers and deep gratitude to those moved to share her work widely.

She is thrilled to be doing what she's here to do—sharing inspired poetry with the world and this pitcher will not stop pouring so stay tuned!

Made in the USA
Columbia, SC
10 June 2022

61426630R00167